Introduction

"So what are you guys trying to do here?" I think that's what Rick asked Mark and me. The three of us sat at a table at Cunningham's in Kearney, Nebraska. I'm pretty sure an order of Tater Nachos was also in attendance. Mark and I had solicited Rick's advice as we approached the conclusion of the rough draft phase of writing this book. Rick is a gifted teacher. He is a talented writer. He has been published many times over. And he is a great friend who wouldn't pull any punches when it came to a critique of what Mark and I had put to paper. In short, Rick would tell us if we had dirt on our faces (more on that later in the book).

Rick talked us through marketing, themes, organization, and logistics. We seemed to be getting hung up on how to organize the work into sections. After some roundabout discussion interrupted by mouthfuls of Tater Nachos, Rick finally brought things to a culmination with, "So what are you guys trying to do here?"

If memory serves me correctly I said, "This book isn't about sections. It's not driven by a prescribed systemic implementation program. It's about what has worked for us. When people pick it up, I want them to find some skills they can use. I want them to find stories they can relate to. I want them to identify with the thinking behind why these things are important. This isn't going to be a book outlining a step-by-step process. It's going to be something that when you pick it up and read a section, your day is going to be better because you learned something, or it enhanced what you already do, or it validated why what you do is important, or motivated you to keep doing what's important. That's what we are trying to do, Rick."

I stepped down off my soapbox, took a breath, and

contemplated another bite of Tater Nachos.

Rick has this telling smile that makes an appearance every now and then. It's a good thing when it shows up. It's like a marker for some about to be expressed enlightenment from a Zen master. Now was one of those times. "That goes at the front of your book. Just let people know that up front and everything else falls into place."

So now you all know as well. We hope this book does all those things for you. We hope it's what you need when you need it. Thanks for having enough belief that it can be.

It Happens In The Hallway - Sam Stecher

18 to 114. I counted the steps today. 18 steps from the front door of my school to the nearest classroom and 114 steps to the farthest. I spend a lot of time thinking about what happens in those steps.

17. That's how many years I have served in this school district. I've served in 8 different positions in 7 buildings, 8 classrooms, and 5 offices.

A number I have lost track of - The number of trainings, programs, inservices, etc I have attended. Some of the trainings not only stuck with me, but fundamentally changed how I viewed education, behaved as an educator, interacted with my students, and collaborated with my fellow professionals. Other training sessions seemed more like time served as opposed to enhancing my service. We have all been in those trainings. They can be a repackaging of what we already know or too much new information to digest and implement in the time allotted. Often they are viewed as the "one more thing on our plate" that as teachers we simply do not have the time, energy, funding, or space to manage.

Through all those trainings, both noble and misguided, one thing was always constant – 18 to 114. Not those specific numbers, but the steps themselves. No matter what, I was going to walk in the door to my classroom or office. No matter the content, students, role, or facility I was going to have to take those steps and cover the distance. I have been expected to implement, monitor, and document numerous interventions. I couldn't do any of it without first taking that walk from door to door. And that isn't the only walk. Everyday classroom to classroom to office to copy room to cafeteria to media center and so on are part of our routine.

What happens during those steps?

With next to no extra steps, time, or training it can become an incredibly impactful event. You don't need a special certification. You won't need to document your efforts and submit them for evaluation. You just need to be aware and intentional during those steps. Who do you see? How do you interact with them? So much can happen in those 18 to 114 steps. The value of our school community culture is largely determined but what happens in our hallway. More specifically, how we decide to carry ourselves, how we choose to interact, during that walk.

Walk down the hallway differently. You are taking those steps anyway. Make a plan for who you see during those 18 to 114 steps.
During that walk I'm going to ask one student what is the most important thing they learned this week.
During that walk I am going ask at least one peer what has been the best part of her day.
During that walk nobody is getting by me without a high five.

Have you ever heard that cliche about it's not the destination, but the journey? You take hundreds of tiny journeys every week. Don't let those journeys be idle steps that serve no other purpose beyond getting from car to classroom. What we do in our classrooms is essential to our school community climate. I know you are intentional, purposeful, and planned in your classrooms. Without what you do in the classrooms we would fall apart as school communities.

But it happens in the hallway, too. It happens on our sidewalks and sidelines. It happens on our playgrounds and parking lots. And it can happen without adding to your plate. It can happen without demanding upon your other resources of time, funding, and energy. Actually, I am of the belief that deciding to carry yourself with a mission as you take those steps will give you more energy and enhance the time you have available.

Those steps are an inherent resource. It is not a resource that can be banked for another day. With each footfall they are expended. Spend them in a manner that reinvests back into your classrooms, students, and peers. It is not a quantifiable investment. I've yet to determine how we measure what we do in those 18 to 114 steps.

In my heart I know that the impact of what we do during those journeys is important beyond measure. 18 to 114. We can all count those steps. More importantly, we can all make those steps count.

For Some Students School Is The "One Best Place" -
Sam Stecher

Andrew, a fellow educator and friend of mine, likes to ask
people what has been the best part of their day. It is subtly
but profoundly different from the ubiquitous "How are you
today?" Instead of getting the tired and worn out reply of
"Fine" you often get a pause followed by some reflection
which leads to a smile accompanied by an honest answer.
Once I picked this up from Andrew it truly became one of
little things I delighted in on a daily basis.

As a rule, the younger you are, the better you are at
answering. It is just the way some things are in life. Once
you get past 12 years of age you have left your best years
of sandbox play and "knock knock" jokes behind. It is
nearly impossible to enjoy a grilled cheese sandwich at 30
as much as you did when you were 8. When you are in
your 40s and somebody asks you what has been the best
part of your day you might pause, reflect, and gently reply
that you feel rather "regular" today. But if you ask a 5 year
old, "What has been the best part of your day?" you
instantly turn that child into a rock star with a complete
performance set list of everything awesome that has
happened that day like-

"Mommyletmepickoutmyownsockssoipickedsomeofdaddys
an
dtheygouppastmykneesandigotanowieonmykneebutthesoc
ks
makeitksolhadthefloatycerealforbrafasttodayandthistime
whenlshareditwithmycatmycatdidn'tpukeornothingandsol
thoughtnextyearforHalloweenlcanbeacatwithlongsocksthat
doesn'tpukecuaselbetacatthatdoesntpukewouldgetawhole

bunchofcandyandstuff."

For real.

So I ask my students what has been the best part of their day quite a bit. On Mondays I frequently ask what was their favorite part of the weekend. Same idea. Different words. One day I applied that line of questioning to three of my 5th Graders.
The answers were as follows:
- Playing Video Games
- Fishing With My Dad
- Coming Back to School

For the most part those were pretty straight forward and expected. But that third answer, it had some baggage. Of course as a principal I am excited when one of my students thinks that highly of school, when returning to school after the weekend is anticipated eagerly. Unfortunately for this young man, his excitement about school had a background that wasn't so positive.

He called school his "one best place." Why? The why has two parts. The first part is that home was an ugly place for him to be. One of my great frustrations in serving students and families as an educator is the all too common occurrence of finding my students in a circumstance that is consistently unhealthy, but not dire enough to intervene in the manner my idealist heart desires. A child's home can have the heat on, food in the fridge, and a child saying he feels safe, when in fact, it is not safe to my standards. He might even withhold information for years in order to protect the only thing he knows as "family" even if it is decidedly unhealthy. Some homes are an ugly place where what gets fostered is the ability to cope and survive and little else. I am not going to get into the details of what was wrong with this child's home. If you have served a child like this you know.

But the second part of why the best part of his weekend was coming back to school was because school was the best place he had. School was his *one best place*. It was where he found empathy, support, love, expectations, compliments, consequences, laughter, role models, friends, smiley face potatoes, recess, knowledge, second chances, guidance, books, dreams, consistency, silliness, clubs, singing, and scooter hockey.

One Spring as our school year was coming to a close, I had a conversation with my father. He made a comment about how excited my students must be for the summer vacation. I said, "Well Dad, we have a handful that are pretty stressed about it." Summer meant they no longer had access to the safe and stable place school provided for them. This flummoxed my Father. The notion that summer could be anything other than a time to be eagerly anticipated by a kid was completely foreign to him. In his experience school was fine, but it just couldn't compete with the privileges of Summer. But my Dad had a safe and loving home where he grew up. So did I. Not so for every child we serve.

My Father gained a new perspective, and I hope it is one we all keep. Please keep in mind I am sure all of you serve some amazing families. I bet most of the homes we send our students to are great places to grow up, with parents that do absolutely the best they can with the love and resources they have. I am so fortunate to have so many parents taking great care of the students I serve. With the vast majority of families I serve they are on the same team with the school collaborating for the success of their children. But for some of our students, school is the best thing they have. Don't ever lose sight of that. School wouldn't be that "one best place" were it not for everything the adults in the building do. Keep it up. It's worth it. You are part of that "one best place" for the child that needs it.

Fake It Until You Make It - Sam Stecher

It wasn't long ago I was in the midst of what is commonly called the "Abagnale Phase" of a new career. And by commonly called, I mean just me really. I'm the only one that calls it that. So it's not common vernacular at all. But I think it could be a thing. Like a thing people say as a commonly understood colloquialism. Or at least maybe something that attains Urban Dictionary status. I'm guessing that as you read this most of you do not have a notion that pops in your head associated with the Abagnale Phase. No visual. No shared experience. Nothing where you go "Oh Lord, I remember this one Abagnale Phase. I wasn't even sure I knew how to batter fish anymore." You know more about it than you think. Chances are you have a context for the cultural reference as well as the experience. If you have lived through any change or challenge you've had your very own Abagnale Phase.

The Cultural Reference - Ever hear of a little movie called "Catch Me If You Can?" It's got a couple of fellas named Leonardo DiCaprio and Tom Hanks in it. Maybe you've heard of them. Here is short plot synopsis if you missed it: Leo plays a con man. Tom plays the cop trying to catch him. Leo's character's speciality is pretending to be something he's not. He pretends to be an airline pilot. In doing so he spends a lot of time in airports, on planes, and in the company of pilots. He also assumes the roles of a doctor and a lawyer. Again he keeps company with people that ought to be able to detect his deception but he manages to pull off the charade. He never flies a plane or practices medicine. He just acts like he knows what he's doing and people buy it. What's really compelling is that this is based on a real guy named Frank Abagnale. Google that dude. It's a pretty amazing story.

The Experience - Three years ago I began serving as an elementary principal. Prior to that I had taught at a middle school for eleven years and served as a high school Dean of Students for three years. Notice that experience didn't include any time at an elementary school. I had been successful in my previous roles. I had a lot of assets suited for both roles preceding the principalship. Going into an elementary experience wasn't an asset I possessed. I had so much to learn before I could say with any confidence that I knew what I was doing, let alone call myself proficient. About 6 weeks in, my boss stopped by for a little evaluatory conversation. When asked how it was going I told him that I felt like Frank Abagnale. Frank (Leo's character) wasn't good at being a doctor or pilot or attorney. He was good at pretending he knew what he was doing. He was good at convincing the people around him he was those things. I felt as though I wasn't even close to being good at being an elementary principal. But I had gotten pretty decent at pretending to be a principal. It was my hope I would learn what I needed to do before too many people noticed. Maybe not the best thing to tell your boss but he seemed to understand.

I was in what I later started to call my Abagnale Phase of a new job. And upon reflection I realized I went through an Abagnale Phase as a teacher. I would suppose that most of us spent some amount of time standing in front of the students enrolled in our first classes "faking it" for lack of a better term. I can remember a veteran teacher telling me that since I wasn't endorsed in middle school, English, or math (which was of course my teaching assignment) that I should "fake it until you make it." I think she may have added that if I didn't pull that off my students might eat me alive. So fake it I did. I pretended that I knew what I was doing. And eventually, minute by minute, class by class, I quit faking it because I settled in. I learned what I needed to know. I learned how to use my skills and talents to do what needed to be done. Faking it became making it and eventually it became thriving.

When I interviewed for the Dean of Students position, one of the interviewers, the principal actually, started the interview by saying, "The job description you were shown isn't what you will be doing. We are not exactly sure what your duties will be. We will sort that out if you get the job." New job + First time in administration + My potential boss isn't even sure of my responsibilities = Abagnale Phase for sure.

I think that any time you really challenge yourself, a bit of faking it is required. At some point you have to do something you've never done before, put on the cloak of confidence, and say "I got this." As I started serving as a superintendent of schools I realized wrapped up in this position would be the roles of director of human resources, curriculum and instruction, finance, and transportation. Leonardo DiCaprio help me, Abagnale Phase in panic mode.

But you know what? This Abagnale Phase phase I've coined, this notion of faking it until you make it, we have another word for it. It's called learning. Every time we ask our students to do something beyond their proficiency level or comfort zone, we are asking them to fake it just a bit because we as educators know it's a necessary step to making it. If we just rest on what we know, on what we are comfortable with, and get further and further from those times we had to fake it, we lose touch with the experience of learning we so often ask of our students.

I've got a lot of learning to do. Call it "fake it until you make it" or the Abagnale Phase. Either way, it's learning for sure. And really, that should be the real reason everyone goes to school, new superintendents included.

The Continuum of Education: Are you a Bump or Dip?
- Mark Johnson

Think back to your school days. Try to remember your teachers, your friends, the subjects you had throughout the day. Chances are you do remember some things about that time in your life; some positive, some negative. You know you learned something during all those years of school. You had to have learned something; otherwise the teachers wouldn't have passed you on to the next grade. But what did you learn? I bet the specifics elude you. For example, I bet you can still do long division, but you probably don't remember which teacher introduced it to you or how that skill was taught to you.

I remember my third grade teacher. Her name was Mrs. Wallingford. She was the first girl I ever had a crush on. She had auburn hair that bounced on her shoulders, and always wore just a little too much rouge. I would have walked through fire for her. One day she announced we would have a contest: the boy and girl who tested on their multiplication facts the fastest would get to go bowling with her one night after school. That was absolutely the only motivation I needed. It wasn't long before I was at the local alley trying to impress her with a strike.

Here are some other things I can recall from elementary school: I got my first kiss on the cheek from a girl named Shelby in first grade. In fourth grade, I attempted to show a card trick for the talent show, but it completely bombed. In fifth grade, I remember being the editor of the school newspaper, and also getting my name written on the board for throwing an eraser. In sixth grade, I melted crayons on the radiator, and got a zero on a Weekly Reader Quiz for showing my answers to the little blonde girl sitting next to me.

So what is the point of all this rambling? Only to convey this message: I learned a lot of academics in this process but I can't pinpoint what I learned in most grades (except, of course, for the multiplication facts). And when I was a teacher, I wasn't so naïve to think that the students I had each year would remember everything that I taught them. However, I did know the curriculum I taught each year was vitally important. I also knew learning goals were important, and I wrote them on the board so my students could see exactly what we would be learning each day. I taught routines, procedures, rules, math, reading, writing, social studies, etc.

I also introduced my students to Elvis Presley and played his music throughout the day.
When my past students see me, they don't thank me for teaching them about the Revolutionary War. They don't write me letters praising my ability to teach them the associative property. What they do is usually as me this question: "Hey Mr. Johnson, do you still listen to Elvis?"

In fact, just a few months ago, I ran into a student at the mall that I haven't seen for over 10 years. After we took some time to catch up and talk about the old times, he said this to me. "You know, Mr. Johnson, I don't remember anything you taught me in 5th grade. But I do remember two things perfectly. One, you gave us all nicknames, and mine was Dr. Evil. And two, one day the class asked you how you got your hair to look so good everyday. And you said, 'Well kids, every morning when I wake up, I look in the mirror and say, Wow, you are one handsome devil.'"

This encounter with an old student couldn't have proved my point any better.

What I have come to realize is that the educational process is a continuum. As a teacher, you fall somewhere along that continuum. When the students reach you, they will either have a positive or a negative experience. I call it either a "bump" or a "dip" along the continuum. It's your job as a teacher to make sure that the students hit a bump.

How do you become a bump? Simply put, you build positive, intentional relationships with your students. You let them into your world, and you find a way to get into theirs. You try and make every day count. You build traditions with them in your classroom, and make memories they will carry forever. You teach them to think, to dream, to reach for their goals, to get up when they get knocked down, and to have faith in themselves and each other. They might not remember exactly what you taught them, but they will remember that their 5th grade teacher was the "bomb" and always wore a tie and told funny jokes to start the day. And this memory might have been the thing that kept them going when things got tough.

It boils down to this: Do whatever you can to be a bump on the continuum for your students, because otherwise you will be a dip. And no one wants to be a dip.

Everyday Life Saving Measures - Sam Stecher

After one of our all too common incidents of school violence I received a Facebook message from one of my former coaches. The quote follows unedited. Warning - It does a have just a bit of salty language.

"I was reading about how it was an Assistant Principal who took down the kid who was stabbing people at the Pennsylvania high school today and in my head the asst principal was you. You would totally stop a stabbing spree, possibly with an arm bar. Thanks for being a badass that is keeping our schools safe."

I get these on occasion. It's not uncommon for me to receive these kinds of messages. People have described my build as that of lavatory constructed of masonry. Most of my friends engage in golf as a recreational activity. I elect to compete in tournaments where the objective is to twist the limbs of my opponent in such a manner that they are left with the options of conceding defeat or suffer joint dislocation. Husbands of teachers I serve with have told me they feel more secure in the safety of their spouses at school because "a guy like you" is the principal. I realize I have a bit of reputation and an image that lends itself to this. But it's not like I am Liam Neeson starting my morning announcements with "Hello. This is your principal, Mr. Stecher. I have a very particular set of skills, skills I have acquired over a very long career, skills that make me a nightmare for people that want to mess with my school." The schools I have served are very safe places. However, it has very little to do with the imposing figure I may or may not present. I and everybody I serve with does do something very intentional on a consistent basis that makes our school inherently safer. It has nothing to do with metal detectors, security guards, or lock down drills. It has everything to do with what I learned and what I continue to learn from someone who lived and led through one of our worst nightmares.

When Bill Bond has something to say I listen. If you are not familiar with Bill, he is a School Safety Specialist working with the National Association of Secondary Principals. He was also the Principal of Heath High School, the site of the school shooting in Paducah, Kentucky in 1997. I have seen Bill speak on several occasions. I have spoken of him multple times on the MissionMonday.com podcast. So much of what I practice proactively and reactively in crisis situations I learned from Bill. You can call it hyperbole but I will stand behind the statement - What I have learned from Bill Bond saves lives.

I once listened to an interview with Bill discussing if our schools were safer based on the lessons we have learned and the interventions put in place post Columbine. Bill was very blunt in stating that measures such as Zero Tolerance Policies and Metal Detectors do not make the difference in preventing acts of violence upon our schools. What he did say worked was trust. In a very candid quote, Bill stated of his own experience with tragedy at Heath High, "What could have prevented it in Paducah and prevented it in many other places - if students had trusted the adults, had trusted the adults with the information that he had a gun at school the day before, that he was talking about - stay away from the lobby, something big is going to happen. Many students knew something was going to happen, and no one told."

He goes on to say Zero Tolerance Policies are actually an obstacle to establishing those trusting relationships. Instead of focusing on Zero Tolerance we should be focusing on building an environment of trust between all of our school community stakeholders. I have long held this belief, but Bill brought to light an aspect that had eluded me. I had been focused on finding those students we would describe as "at risk," fostering trusting relationships, and being an adult that made a difference in how they perceived school. And if it wasn't me, I wanted to facilitate another adult in reaching out to those "at risk" students. The reality that Bill addresses is that despite our best efforts we won't bond with every student. It is a tragic fact, but we do serve students that a for multitude of complex reasons will resist heartfelt, determined, and consistent efforts on our part to bond. I lose sleep over it but it is true. On occasion we do all that we can and fail. But it's the exception, not the rule. All those times we succeed in bonding a child, any child, to school we are engaged in a life saving measure. Bill needed just one student to let an adult at school know something wasn't right. If just one student had said something to someone they trusted with the ability to set the right course of action in motion, lives could have been saved. What Bill made me realize is that though I may fail to reach that one student, I can build a trusting relationship with scores of students every year. Every one of those relationships is someone who might say, "Mr. Stecher, I don't want to get anybody in trouble but..." There is no effort made towards fostering positive bonding to the school community that is a waste. I am humbled but the fact that I will fail at connecting with some student who desperately needs that connection. I know it's happened in the past. I know that it will happen again. But another successful relationship may provide the grace we need.

Going back to the previous correspondence from my coach my response was, "Thanks, Coach. Glad you have that faith in me. But more importantly everyone I serve with works so so hard to make sure we give all our students a reason to love the school, to love the people in it, and to know that they are loved and valued by us. I can think of no better preventative measure."

We work to do this for all our students. We may not reach all. But the bonds we do foster may save the ones we didn't connect with.

The Myth of Digital Citizenship and Why We Need to Teach It Anyway - Sam Stecher

At one time in the not so distant past there were no cell phones. And then everything changed at a rate faster than the speed of amending a student handbook. I can distinctly remember the first time one of my 8th grade students brought a cell phone to school. It really wasn't that big of a deal, more of a novelty really. I mean, one student with a cell phone had next to no bearing on our day-to-day school operations. But then a second student brought a cell phone. That gave every 8th grade student license to go home and lament to mother and father that everybody else had one and they were the only student without what had become the essential accessory. Mother and father, worn down by this insistence and wooed by the safety rationales, relented. 8th grade cell phone possession became the norm. And that's when my fellow teachers lost their minds.

We had no specific rule established for cell phone use. And the students were all tangled up in this new fangled texting thing. So we had meetings addressing the texting crisis. I shall paraphrase the meeting dialog:

"Sam, they are texting each other. They are texting each other in class."
I didn't see the problem the same way my peers did.
"Um, isn't this kinda just like passing notes?"
"No Sam, it isn't. This is new technology. This is a problem."
"I get that it's new technology. But aren't we talking about basically the same behavior? We've just shifted from an analog to a digital method, right? I'm thinking I would

probably handle this pretty much like any other classroom distraction."

"Sam, it's like you didn't hear us. This isn't passing notes. This. Is. Texting."

It made me wonder. In the 19th Century, with the advent of mass produced pencils and paper granting students previously unrealized liberties with stationary and writing instruments, did educators find themselves re-evaluating their expectations in order to manage the disruption brought about by such technological advances? My intuition tells me yes. As educators, this guy included, we tend to overthink things occasionally. I'm thinking that they established a finite paper allocation and a pencil check out system. Maybe even a cart rolling up and down the hall that housed the pencils when not in use.

We tend to forget that if we teach clear and comprehensive expectations about behavior, we have pretty much all our technology bases covered in regard to digital citizenship. Why? The reason is because there is no such thing as digital citizenship. *It's just citizenship.* The rules don't change just because you have a screen in front of you.

Fast forward to my time as Dean of Students at a high school. Before the school year, multiple teachers and administrators met as a behavior and security committee. One of the issues we addressed was our cell phone use expectation. The prevailing opinion of the committee members was an "Off and Out of Sight" policy as in, prior to entering the school building students were required to power off the cell phones and keep them out of sight until the last bell of the school day. This was in 2008 in a school of 1500 students. We were proposing an expectation that for all intents and purposes required cell phones to not exist between the hours of 8:10 AM to 3:20 PM within our walls. This seemed unreasonable and unrealistic to me. I voiced that instead, we teach responsible cell phone use consistent with our other behavior expectations. That didn't happen. Which meant that in my first year as Dean, I invested a fair amount of time into cell phone policing. Since I have departed that position, someone more persuasive than I convinced the powers that be to adopt what I would call a more reasonable policy based on responsible use of personal digital devices (who says cell phone anymore anyway?) as opposed to near prohibition. What I am saying is that the students by in large can use such devices at school. Even with what some would term a more lax policy, the students continue to graduate. In fact, they are getting into college. I'm assuming they are taking their smartphones to college with them.

We already had the appropriate policies and expectations in place. All we needed to do is teach how the expectations applied to the technology. That's an important clarification. I think that often when I tell people that there is no such thing as digital citizenship they think that I am advocating ignoring the presence and impact of technology. Nope, that's not it at all. Anytime we gain access to new technology, the potential for misuse is just so appealing. Some of our students will gravitate towards those uses because they are such fun. Without a doubt we need to address these concerns. However, it doesn't need to be wholesale policy change.

How would a good citizen handle this technology? Is your use respectful, responsible, and safe? That's it. That's all you need. For example, "Before you take that picture of yourself with your smartphone and post it on social media, would you take the same picture with a Polaroid camera and walk up and down the halls handing copies out?" Admittedly you might need to explain what a Polaroid is, but you get my drift.

The real way technology challenges us is the impact of misbehavior. The scope and reach is immediate and vast. An infraction that in the analog world would constitute a small gaff can become a full blown media incident in our digital age. What technology has done is taken the social consequences and amplified them beyond the capacity of many of our students to comprehend. It's taken what historically has been pretty low price tag infractions and inflated them at a rate many of us are unprepared to deal with. Consequences we engineer should teach. The consequences brought about by the ramifications of misuse of technology often do not teach. They often do damage. We really have very little control of the coarse reaction the world drops on our children.

What it hasn't changed is how a good person conducts themselves. Teaching and reinforcing how we want our student to conduct themselves is absolutely within our control. Keep teaching those expectations. Focus on the core character principles you want to foster in your students. Don't be scared of the technology access. Know that we probably can't anticipate what innovation will bring next. Technology and progress will not slow its pace. Chances are the fundamental values of citizenship will address it no matter what. Don't rest on teaching good citizenship as part of all interactions. Expect the same conduct face-to-face and screen-to-screen and biotech interface-to-biotech interface. Teaching our students attributes like compassion and empathy and responsibility addresses our digital dilemmas, even the ones we haven't seen yet.

Second Hand Compliments - Sam Stecher

I once read the most insidious force in the universe is gossip. A similar sentiment has been expressed many places, though its original attribution has eluded my research efforts. But the who and when of its origins are not the things that matter. What matters, at least to me, is the realization it brought to me about culture and climate of a school community.

Have you ever walked in on a conversation where - surprise surprise- you were the topic of some less than flattering comments? Or maybe you were on the other end of that scenario - the one dishing the dirt. In either case, that seemingly little interaction causes what could be irreparable damage to the relationship.

Case in point on a grand scale in my little state of Nebraska: Our head football coach at the big university was caught on tape in a very passionate manner expressing some negative perceptions about fans and reporters. By passionate, I mean he used some profanity. A lot really. Including the big one. He dropped it a lot, my friends. There are many facets and substantial debate about how this recording came about and what it means to those invested. But what I want you to know about this little snafu is that he caused significant damage to a boatload of relationships in less than two minutes of commentary he intended for next to nobody to hear. All unintentional. All by accident.

But what if we did this on purpose? And what if it was positive commentary? Not the dropping "f bombs". That is not what I am advocating. What I am advocating is speaking about people when they are not around in a manner that builds them up. Speaking well of the people you serve and the people you serve with in their absence can harness that insidious power normally attributed to the negative, and re-purpose it for a positive culture change. I am not talking about random acts of kindness. This is too important to leave to a random intervention. It needs to be be intentional and consistent.

Accidentally overheard negative comments are extremely destructive. The simple act of engaging in such conversation is destructive, overheard or not. We need to consistently compliment and acknowledge those around us, even when they are not within earshot. Strike that - Especially when they are not around to hear it. I have also heard it said that character is how you behave when nobody is looking. Let's choose our character. Let's model the kind of character we teach and aspire to achieve.

Recently I had 5th grader tell me how good of a goalie one of the 3rd grade students was. She was not around to hear the compliment. The 5th grader just wanted to express something positive about a fellow student. That feels like a pretty positive climate/character indicator to me.
Where do we go with this information? I think this can be big, my friends. Like global impact big. Like a spark that starts as a mission intervention and spreads to a movement. What can you do? Commit to having those conversations in which "Second Hand Compliments" take place. Make it part of who you are. Share this concept with your peers. Like I said, global impact, but it happens one person and one interaction at a time. You are one of those people.

And I bet if this becomes part of who you are it won't be long before you walk into the teacher's lounge and catch somebody saying something nice about you.

"You are in Big Trouble!" - Mark Johnson

Consequences. They seem to be one of those rare constants in life: everything has consequences. A result of an action or a choice we have made will lead to a consequence. Although there can be positive consequences for our choices, the word more often has a negative connotation to it.

In school, we usually give consequences to students who don't follow the rules or meet the expectations set before them. Some of these consequences are quick and easy. For example, if a student doesn't have a pencil for a class where one is needed, a consequence might be that he has to ask to borrow one from someone else, or pay the teacher with "collateral" in order to use one. Another example is homework. A student who doesn't turn in her homework on time might have the consequence of staying in at recess or after school to finish it. Some teachers might even dock points on the assignment for it being turned in late.

But sometimes, the consequences we give students are harder to come by. For example, I recently worked with a student who stole something from the Book Fair, and when confronted, lied about doing it. When his mother came to school to discuss the situation, she was immediately upset and began to dole out consequences for her child, which included kicking him out of school for two weeks and taking him to the police station. This may sound excessive, but without a doubt this mom wanted what is best for her child. However, her reaction, though done out of love, was not leading to the consequences that would do the most teaching, in my opinion. She needed to hear that great kids sometimes just make not so great choices. She needed to hear that if we work together, we can find the consequence that might help change the behavior and get her child back on the right path. Hearing those things lead to a switch being flipped in her perspective. What was on the way to being more of a thrashing than a teachable moment quickly became a productive dialog between parent, child, and principal.

So what is the right thing to do in these situations? We all have handbooks that have lists of infractions and consequences that seem to match the misbehavior. But is that always the best way? It might be the easiest, but is it the BEST?

It is important to remember that the root of the word discipline is "disciple," as in somebody who is guided by the the path and advice of a mentor. When we discipline the children we serve, do our actions provide a path and guidance for the future, or just punishment for the present? We want to help them make good choices and see the value in living a positive life. The best way to do that might not be to simply and swiftly dole out consequences. We should model it so the child learns a lesson from it and changes the behavior, all the while building a positive relationship with them.

After all, isn't that what we really want?

The Power of Saying "O.K." - Mark Johnson

Let's say your child is playing with toys on the living room floor and you would like them picked up so they can get ready for bed. There are many strategies a parent can implement in this situation. One of them involves giving the students a choice: "You can pick up your toys in five minutes or in ten minutes. You choose." One of them involves establishing consequences. "When you go to bed, any of the toys you pick up you get to keep. Any toys left behind, I get to keep." These are both great options when working with your child on how to make decisions when asked to do a task, and giving them some power in the process.

However, it also makes a lot of sense to teach your child how respond to disappointment, and perhaps one day even adversity. Giving your kiddo choices is one way *you* can respond when your child isn't so quick to follow instructions. When you lay out the consequences ahead of time, that is *your* response. Isn't it awesome when it's the child that has the response which then eliminates the need for you to respond? I think so. I think it so awesome we should actually be teaching it.

One of the simplest things you can teach a child to say is "O.K." when you ask them to do something. It would sound like this:
"Hey buddy, I need you to pick up your toys and get ready for bed."
"OK."
See how that works? Let's try that again:
"Honey, it's time to pick up your toys and put them away. Bed time is in ten minutes."

"OK."

Did you get that? The child is still making a choice: to comply or not to comply. The child is deciding if they want to whine, or negotiate for more time, or just simply ignore you. And if whining starts, or negotiations, then you are finding yourself in an argument and getting frustrated and laying on consequences. However, if all you hear is "OK" and the task gets started immediately, then all of those arguments and frustrations go out the door. But just expecting this magical "OK" doesn't make it very likely to happen. You need to put the time into teaching it. If you know your teenager is going to be asking for an extended curfew on Friday night, start early in the week - "Hey, I know on Friday night you have some big plans but we have some work around the house I need help with on Saturday morning. So I might say 11:00 or I might say 11:30 for your curfew, but either way I'm going to need you to just say OK." I also think it a good idea to start teaching the "OK" response way before the teenage years. Think small. Small children and small issues. If you start when both the kiddos and the issues are small, it's more likely the big ones won't become big problems.

This works in a classroom, too. Especially when you need to give a consequence. If an assignment is not turned in, and you say, "Carson, you'll need to stay inside for recess and complete this assignment" (or whatever it is), and the student responds with "OK," then it's done and you both can move on.

That's the power of "OK." It's not about the last word, or fighting for your cause, or making an excuse, or putting blame on others. It's a chance for a child to keep disappointment in perspective and maybe to save us adults some sanity. Even if it means just one less fight, I think that would be pretty OK.

What Works When Consequences Won't - Sam Stecher

Once while sitting at my gate in Midway Airport I had a bit
of an epiphany. It was an alchemy of behavior and
consequences and security checkpoints and relationships
and stand by status. I don't understand the why of the
epiphany. It just presented itself as a self evident truth
seen through the lens of an unintentional case study years
in the making.

The epiphany? When consequences fail to alter behavior,
then relationships just might. Intuitively I knew this, but my
friend and coauthor Mark gave me a pretty profound
example.
For this to make sense you need to know that Mark hates
being on time. If he is at a scheduled event early it makes
him physically uncomfortable. He gets a bit twitchy and
agitated. It's like his brain is sending the message, "Why
are we here? Don't you know we could have been late?
We love being late!" In the rare occurrence where he finds
himself ready to arrive in a timely manner he will actively
find distractions that will delay his departure. It is weird. So
very weird. For as long as I have known him he has been
this way.

For years I have told Mark that if placed in a circumstance
where his tardy disposition collided with an inflexible
timeline I would be more than willing to leave him behind.
After all, I do know all the stories he tells to get his point
across. I have even practiced telling them a few times.
Honestly, I am not quite as engaging, approachable, and
disarming as he. But I get pretty close. I always wondered -
If push came to shove and Mark's insistence on avoiding a
timely arrival did cost him in some capacity, would it

change his extremely ingrained behavior? One day the fates provided me with the answer.

After a presentation in Nashville, Mark and I elected to get to the airport 45 minutes before departure. Though it was a joint decision, I may have arrived sooner were I not in the company of Mark. Mark, on the other hand, was delighted with such a tight timeline. If you are the kind of person to seek advice, let me give you my two cents - When departing from Nashville, 45 minutes is not nearly enough time to take care of business at the airport. We soon began to realize our chances of making our flight were rapidly diminishing from slim to none. Then a minor miracle happened. I was randomly selected for additional security screening. This was only a minor miracle because I get selected for additional security checks with some regularity. Perhaps it is because I am not quite as engaging, approachable, and disarming as Mark. The supplemental security check went rather quickly and it cut me to the front of the line. I made it through just in time to hear the last call page over the intercom for Mark and I to report to our gate. I ran and just made the flight and my connection in Chicago. Mark languished in a line moving at a glacial rate and did not.

I left my good friend Mark in Nashville.

There are so many more details regarding how the rest of the day went, involving everything from stand by flights to pilots shooting the gap between storm cells to groveling at the feet of airline ticket agents. The short version is I arrived home a good six hours before Mark. Mark and I maintained contact throughout this ordeal. This is interesting part - Mark never once expressed concern or stress about how late he would be arriving home or trepidation over the uncertainty of getting bumped from standby on flight after flight. Never once did he say, "I just wish we had been at the airport sooner." What did he say? "This is great. I got this whole standby flight thing figured out, man!"

Let me translate that for you. All the consequences of missing a flight (getting bumped and rerouted multiple times, finding his way home to his family hours later than expected with so much prep work to do in order to be ready for school on Monday) did not make Mark want to change his ways and arrive to an airport or really anyplace early. Instead, his logic led him to the conclusion that he can be so late that he can miss a pretty big deal, like a flight, and still have the tools to deal with it. He, if anything, is even more comfortable being late than ever before. Six hours of consequences did not deter his resolve. His warped brain found a way to validate his behavior.

But here is the deal - Mark shows up on time a lot. Mostly this happens when he knows it is important to someone else (for example, his business partner). He hates it, but he does it. He shows up on time not because of the consequences but because of the relationship he has with others invested. Why do relationships alter his behavior, but not consequences? I do not know. Ulysses Everett McGill once said only a fool looks for logic in the chambers of the human heart. I think the answer is somewhere in there.

This got me thinking. How often with our own students and children do we think that we are not altering behavior because the consequences are not substantial or severe enough? There are some behaviors so ingrained, no amount of consequences can alter the manifestation of said behaviors. Looking for and applying bigger consequences in some circumstances simply isn't viable. Proactively and intentionally fostering positive relationships isn't a 100% intervention, either. But it seems to me it often has a chance to succeed in those circumstances where consequences fall short. I also happen to believe that when consequences do work, the presence of a positive relationship makes them even more powerful. I think we all at times have gone above and beyond for someone not because of consequences, but because of our relationship with them. The children we serve will do so as well. We just need to give them a reason beyond consequences.

Building these relationships doesn't take any more energy than applying consequences. Don't rest on how important it is do so. The relationships you build might be the one chance for a child to make a change.

Your School's First Impression - Mark Johnson

Have you ever heard that you can tell the climate of a school building within ten minutes after you walk in the front door? I happen to buy into that idea. If you don't believe it, try it sometime. You will know exactly what I mean. And honestly, I don't think it takes ten minutes. It can be done in two or less.

In the book *Blink* by Malcolm Gladwell, he states that more often than not, you make judgments about something within two seconds of exposure, or within the blink of an eye. Think back to a time when you had that certain feeling deep down inside about something or someone, almost immediately. Some people might call it a "gut feeling." However, most people don't act on it right away. They shake it off and try to gather more evidence. After all, can you really know someone within such a short time frame? But you would be surprised about how many times that feeling is right. Because upon further review, many times you find yourself right back where you started.

I am always struck by the feeling I get the moment I walk into any school. Within minutes of stepping in the front door, I start making judgments about the climate of the school. And in most cases, after hours of talking and probing and gathering information, I think my early assessments prove to be pretty accurate. Two recent examples on scheduled school visits:

1.   I was greeted by the secretary with a big smile. She escorted me to the library where I met the principal who had a big, boisterous laugh. She offered some bagels in crumpled paper bags and

introduced some teachers. They had a slideshow prepared to showcase some of the great things they were doing at the school. As the presentation rolled, everyone in the room contributed, chiming in their thoughts and sharing personal stories about the school. There was banter and laughter and honest discussion about the successes and frustrations about teaching. Some students were there, they all knew the mission of the school by heart, and they could even tell me what it meant in their own words. My initial feeling was right: this was a school with an attitude of fun, built upon a culture of collaboration.

2.   I was greeted by a secretary who seemed wary of my presence. She escorted me to a back conference room where I was met by the principal who offered a perfect display of rolls and fruit. As this school's slideshow rolled, each person took his or her turn, carefully following a certain order of speaking. There were also personal stories shared, sprinkled within data and numbers and spreadsheets. Students could recite the academic goals for their classrooms, and knew exactly what percentage they needed to reach by school's end. My initial feeling about this school was also right: this was a school with an attitude of business, built upon a culture of learning.

I'm not implying one school was better than the other. Both schools were doing what they felt was best for kids, and both schools were producing some incredible results. But it got me thinking. How does my school speak to people in the first minutes as they walk in the door? We know our guests, our potential new students, and really everybody who pays us a visit is gathering information both consciously and subconsciously. Our schools are speaking to them as they enter, and based on that initial conversation the brains of our visitors are deciding what this place is all about. Since we know this is happening, it just makes sense we should capitalize on it. We should ask ourselves, "Does the first impression of our school react the values and mission of our school?" If it does not, you will be fighting an uphill battle to change the impression ingrained within those first minutes. How you and your staff greet guests, the displays on the walls, the activities which students are engaged, all contribute to the perception. At any given time the collection of these things should add up to an accurate first impression which reflects just what your school is all about. It's worth knowing this. It is worth making sure your staff and students know this. It make a whole lot of sense to have a conversation with them where you talk about the values of your school and ask, "If this is what we value, what do we want people to see when they arrive so they *understand* what we value?" This way your school's first impression isn't left to chance, but instead it is just one more thing your school does well on purpose.

Parent Teacher Conferences: The 20 Minute Cram Session - Mark Johnson

I remember as a kid waiting for my parents to get home from parent/teacher conferences. I would try and watch TV or read a book or play on the Atari, (probably Asteroids) but I just couldn't concentrate. I was too worried about what my teachers were going to say. Even though I knew exactly what my teachers were going to say. I knew this because they said the same thing every year to my parents. It went something like this: "Mark is doing fine in school. His grades are good. We aren't worried about that. He does, however, talk a lot. Like a lot, a lot. So if you could help us to get him to talk less, that would be amazing."

Then I became a teacher and got to see things from the other side of the table. I remember being very nervous before conferences the first couple of years. I tried to share the right things at the right time. Start with the positives, slide in concerns, end with more positives. Show some work, explain some data, yada yada yada....20 minutes is up.

Then I also became a parent and got to experience conferences again from yet another side of the table. (Apparently this is a three-sided table.) However, this time around I'm much more analytical about the conference. And now, for my high school son and middle school daughter, the conference isn't just with one teacher...it's with four or five. And they are all scrambling for time and reading off their notes and trying to give me a cram session on my kid in 20 minutes, all waiting their turn to talk, while I am equally waiting my turn, and the next thing I hear is "Thank you for coming, Mr. Johnson. Let us know if there's anything we can do to help."

When it comes to parent/teacher conferences, there is no way we can say all what needs to be said in five minutes, ten minutes, or even twenty minutes. It's impossible to share everything about a child within that time frame. There is way too much information to cover from a teacher's perspective, and equally as difficult when parents would also like to share information about things that are happening at home. Neither side should be withholding information about children until conference night, or until report card time, or progress reports, or whatever. I believe we need to be in constant communication with each other. It can be done in a variety of ways: through email, twitter, phone calls, face-to-face, a note in a planner, a text message, etc. The method you choose doesn't matter as much as the actual communication. Sam is fond of saying, "Communication is a bonding experience. It has as much to do with building relationships as sharing information."

Every opportunity you take to share with parents lets them see that their child and their time has value well beyond the two nights set aside for conferences. And if you can, imagine the value parents would see and feel when we care enough to come alongside them, share information, celebrate successes as well as concerns, and ask them to be a part of the journey, all year long. That's the type of relationship that would help make for a very successful year for everyone.

It's About More Than Smarts - Sam Stecher

A gentleman named Jim Stigler did some interesting research regarding how Eastern and Western cultures differ in what to value and praise in their students. In a nutshell, Eastern cultures are more likely to praise perseverance through struggle and Western cultures are more likely to express praise for possession of talent or intelligence. When I was first exposed to this research I found it interesting. It caught my attention and it made an enough of an impression that I was able to recall it later during cocktail conversation. But upon first blush didn't find it compelling. It just seemed exposure to a cultural difference that provoked thought but did not truly make me reflect on my own behaviors.

However, as I interacted with my students I began to realize just how often I praised students for being intelligent when in fact being intelligent had nothing to do with why I should praise the student. Now, don't get it too twisted. My students loved being praised for their smarts. These were positive interactions that fostered healthy productive relationships.

But when I spent my time praising students for being smart, even for academic achievements (and I have done more than my share of praising students as smart for meeting behavior expectations), I should have been praising them for working hard or paying attention or taking risks. In short, I was praising the students for what they possessed; that possession being intelligence. Truth be told sometimes my praise for smarts wasn't always praise for the possession of smarts. It was praise in the hope of instilling a value of intelligence. Rather than praising them for what they had, I should have been praising them for what they did – eliciting behaviors that got the results – especially the behaviors that were a struggle. If we do not praise the struggle that leads to success and only praise the smarts, our students will deduce that struggle equates to a lack of intelligence. And if they believe intelligence is the key, and the struggle indicates they do not have that key, they will be resigned to give up on acquisition of that skill or learning.

So what does this have to do with school culture? Stigler says, "It's hard to do anything that changes culture. But it can be done." He goes on to talk about how we could change our views on what we value in learning. I would propose we really don't have much to change regarding our views. The behaviors that allow students to benefit from struggle are all valued. What we need to do is change our own behaviors. It is easy to praise smarts. It feels good. It has its value for certain. But if we make it a consistent habit to praise the behavior, to praise what they do, instead of praise what they have, we can have a culture change with a real impact. If a student demonstrates honesty, than praise the honest behavior. Explain why the honesty was important. If it was a struggle to tell the truth, praise the student's character. If a student does research to find an answer, praise the act of the research, the dedication, and the resourcefulness. I implore you, do not just say, "How smart of you." We can do better. And if we do better our students will as well.

A True Friend Tells You When You Have Dirt On Your Face - Sam Stecher

I found that sentiment in a fortune cookie. It may sound odd, but in the company of a half full container of Chicken Kung Pao and that tiny slip of paper I was granted a moment of clarity. I like to think that is the intent of all those wisdom bearing cookies, that somewhere in a far off land a wise sage suffers over each syllable before baking the message into a novelty, knowing that someone needs what is contained within. When the sage has the perfect expression of wisdom, an assistant rushes it off to a scribe expressing an urgency knowing that this is all part of destiny's mechanism. Or maybe they just use some sort of app at the fortune cookie factory. Either way it became a formative principle for me.

Early in my teaching career I intuitively knew how important relationships were to the effectiveness of instruction. And before long I had some pretty solid validation of my intuition from peers, mentors, and even an expert or two. Even with that validation I still struggled to define the parameters of what the teacher-student relationship looked like. I heard phrases like "appropriate separation" that tried to approximate the closeness or distance of those relationships, but I found nothing that accurately defined it for me. Then came the take out box of Kung Pao and the accompanying fortune cookie. That was it. "A true friend tells you when you have dirt on your face." That was the relationship I sought with my students. For this to work we have to tweak the word *friend* just a bit. We don't mean friend as in boon companion that one would take on a road trip. Rather we mean someone with whom we have mutual respect.

The part that really resonated with me was *dirt on your face.* You see, in education we are in the business of telling people they have dirt on their faces. I think we forget just how often it is explicitly what we are obligated to do. Two of the most prevalent examples from our profession:

1. Every time you provide input on an assignment that is not 100% correct you are pointing out dirt on someone's face.
2. Every time you correct a behavior that does not meet your expectations you are pointing out dirt on someone's face.

We have to do those things. We have to tell our students when they have dirt on their faces. If our students are metaphorically without dirty faces we would be out of a job.

We have all been in the situation where somebody with whom we lacked the requisite respectful relationship offered us criticism, constructive or otherwise, and it was not well received. In order for such input to be a useful instructional tool, that positive productive relationship is essential. It is equally essential to be intentional in establishing those relationships. If we are giving the criticism on purpose we ought to be establishing the relationships on purpose, too. I implore you, do not rest on this. Be consistently intentional about this. Keep building those relationships. We can't afford to tell our students they have dirt on their faces without it.

Has Anybody Told You You're Awesome Today? - Sam Stecher

I have a question for you. Has anybody told you you're awesome today? I'm actually asking you right now. Has anybody taken the time today to stop and say, "Hey, you're awesome." It's important to me that you know you are. I have no doubt that at some point you have without question inspired awe. If you are an educator or a parent and you put your heart and soul into what you do, I guarantee you inspire awe. And students, no group of people awes me more often than students. So if you haven't heard it yet today let me be the first to tell you. You. Are. Awesome.

I like letting people know that about themselves. I happened upon my affinity for doing so quite by accident. One morning I was performing my hallway supervisor duties and as an 8th grade boy rolled up on me, eyes down, hoody up, rather disengaged from humanity, I paused him in his laborious trek to home room and said, "Hey, has anybody told you you're awesome today?" What possessed me to employ this intervention is beyond me other than it just felt right. Eighth Grade Hoody Boy raised his eyes and with deep introspection and profound befuddlement replied, "Uh...No."
"Well, let me be the first to tell you today. You're awesome."
This garnered a heartfelt, "Um...Thanks."
But as he walked away he paused again after about ten yards, turned back, and gave me that head nod we bros give each other to signal something is legit. You know the nod. One short motion, chin up, subtle yet decidedly

discernible, universally conveying acknowledgement and respect. That head nod.

"For real, Mr. S. Thanks."

I knew it felt right.

Since that time I've made it a habit and on occasion a mission. And you don't have to commit to awesome. Give your students any positive acknowledgment that is legitimate. It's such a good way to validate the behaviors we want to foster.

"Has anybody told you today that you do a great job of following hallway expectations?"

"Has anybody told you today that you're always prepared for class?"

It can even be something you hope they attain.

"Has anybody told you that you could be an amazing doctor someday?"

"Has anybody told you that you could be a great reader someday?"

That last one should sound familiar to the students I presently serve. A gentleman named Aaron Davis stopped by one of our schools last week to share his message with our 7th through 12th graders. One of the things he shared was a story about a teacher in grade school who told Mr. Davis as a child, "You are going to be a great reader someday." This teacher told Mr. Davis what he could accomplish daily without fail. If I remember correctly Mr. Davis also let us know that he happens to be working on his third book. It seems he has surpassed being a great reader. I bet he would validate that somebody specifically and intentionally letting him know what he could be had a lot to do with what he became.

The reactions I get when I say, "Well, let me be the first to tell you…" are the second best thing about informing people of their awesomeness. What's the first best thing? When I inquire, "Has anybody told you you're awesome today?" and the answer I get is, "For sure. Mr. Zimmerman told me that in the hall today. But it's good to hear it from you, too." The only thing better than this little school climate intervention being novel is when such interactions become the norm.

By the way, has anybody told you this could be the norm for your school? If they haven't, permit me the honor of being the first. You could be part of making it the norm. How do I know you have this kind of capability? Word on the street is that you're awesome and this is exactly the kind of thing awesome people do.

Three Things Nobody Tells You About Building Relationships With Your Students - Sam Stecher

When I was an undergrad my teaching methods professor once said, "I get so nervous before I teach this class I feel like I could throw up." That's a pretty solid indicator that maybe she wasn't the best candidate for teaching people how to teach. In fact that quote is the only thing I can remember with any certainty that she actually said. All that accompanied that gem of professorial enlightenment was an absence of truckload of things which should have been said. Once I had my own classroom these became readily apparent. Whenever I am called upon to speak to student teachers, I like to clue them in on three pieces of advice I wish had been part of my teacher education program.

1) Lose The Charisma
To be fair, charisma isn't bad. However, reliance on charisma is. Even worse is using a perceived lack of charisma as an excuse. Too often we attribute the ability to foster positive and productive relationships with students as a result of teachers possessing some unquantifiable and unattainable charisma. But charisma as a classroom climate intervention is a myth. It will be money for the first 20 minutes of class, and maybe even a week if you can really work it. But it isn't sustainable. You might be able to sell your students the Intolerable Acts with the sheer power of your classroom presence, but by the time you get to the Monroe Doctrine they have seen that pony do its one trick. The inherent likability charisma affords you can open the door and make you more accessible to your students. But as I am prone to say, do not rest on that. If you want the relationships you foster with your students to be sustainable and result in learning, you have to engage in

intentional interactions far beyond your affable personality. That trumps charisma every time. Charisma isn't something you can do or plan or decide upon. But intentional interactions? Those you can.

2) Be Relentless With Your Persistence
You know that one kid? The one you have said, "Good Morning" to every day since the beginning of the school year? The one that has ignored you or given you the stink eye every time? Yes, that one. Remember that day you thought he was going to finally say it back, but it was actually just some combination of a stifled sneeze and an indifferent grunt? Keep saying "Good Morning" to him. Make it a priority and do your best to never miss a day. Find out his name and add that to your good morning mix. I have a handful of students that upon first blush, and second blush, and through an epoch and an era or two seemed impervious to my insistent relationship building interventions. It also seems they are the ones that need it the most – the ones it pays off the most for. Some of the students we serve need nine weeks of interventions, sometimes more. We owe it to them.

3) Do Something With Your Visibility
Don't just stand there. Whether it's at the game, on the playground, in the hallway, cafeteria, any place you see your students, don't just supervise. Don't just be seen. If all you do is be seen in those places, eventually you become about as interactive as furniture. I mean, one can interact with furniture, but you really can't have a productive relationship with it. I suppose some people would say you could, but I don't roll with those folk. Engage your students. Have conversations. Give high-fives. Teach a social skill. Ask questions. Tell them about

your favorite burrito. Maybe that last one was a bit specific, but man, the Big City Breakfast Burrito with chorizo sausage is my jam and I love talking about it. I also like to talk about the injustice that is the absence of a lemon-flavored Pop Tart. My point is that this isn't rocket surgery. We all know we are supposed to be out where our students are. Take that next step and do something with that visibility.

4 Habits of Teachers That Have "It" - Part 1 - Eye Contact - Sam Stecher

Do you ever hear educators talk about how some teachers just have "it," whatever "it" may be when it comes to bonding with students? I agree that some teachers do have a certain something, a difficult to define quality, that makes them inherently better at fostering the relationships supporting a positive classroom climate. What I do not agree with is the label many people ascribe to the elusive quality - charisma. Charisma doesn't cut it as a "go to" strategy for classroom management. If you are charismatic it will open the door to positive relationships. But if you rely on it, then enjoy your luck running out in short order. Charisma is a veneer that will be worn through by anything beyond the superficial interactions of what we must do in our day-to-day operations of a school and classroom.

So if it isn't charisma then what is "it"? I am of the belief that "it" is actually three or four habits that, through subtle practice, are performed consistently by teachers that have "it." Mark and I believe that it is important to devote some time to the skills that collectively and consistently trump charisma.

We start with eye contact. Good teachers consistently make eye contact with students, both in the whole classroom setting and in one-on-one interactions. Eye contact is one of the basic ways humans bond. It does us good to remember that research has shown both students and teachers are consistently human. This may seem simple but we live in an age where it is far too easy to disregard eye contact. Early in my teaching career one of the things that distracted me from consistent eye contact was the bright and shiny technological marvel of a computer the school district provided for my classroom use. Once I had my students rolling with independent work I would sit down at the computer and begin to answer emails and enter grades. In doing so, my proximity and my eye contact fell into instant disrepair. For example, when students came to ask me for help with a question, my assistance devolved in an order something like this:

"The answer is one of our three branches of government. I will give you a hint - it is not the one that is responsible for writing the laws. That leaves you with two options. See what you can find and check back with me".....to,

"It's gotta be Legislative, Executive, or Judicial. Look at thedefinitions we wrote yesterday".....to,

"The answer is on page 67".....to,

"The answer is on page 67 in the third paragraph".....to,

"The answer is on page 67 in the third paragraph in bold"..... to,

"Maybe you should skip this one and work on another question."

All the while my attention was focused primarily on the screen and the other tasks I was trying to address so that I could use my plan time to actually plan. What I am saying is that I could rationalize a good intent for my computer but I was for sure dropping the ball. Fortunately, I realized the error of my ways. I moved my computer out of my classroom and into my office. Eliminating what I allowed to be a distraction really made me focus on my eye contact and attention. It was a pretty easy fix once I quit rationalizing and owned up to what I needed to do to get better.

However, things have changed. Instead of one screen in a classroom, everybody has a screen. In some cases we check out a school-issued screen for each student to use. We have a huge screen in most classrooms, and almost everybody is carrying a tiny screen with them that is buzzing and flashing and beeping for attention all the time. The tech companies have us all believing that these are notifications. I wish they would change their vernacular and change the wording in the settings of our phones to say distractions instead of notifications. Now more than ever before we have so many things competing for our attention and eye contact. And I am as guilty as anybody as far as being susceptible to these distractions. I confess that I have on occasion been in the midst of cafeteria supervision when a kindergartener says something so cute I have to tweet it because, you know, because that's a paramount priority, and while I am tweeting I miss who knows how many subtle yet valuable interactions that include eye contact.

All the technology isn't just a distraction. It is an important, borderline essential to what we do as educators. But for all the magic technology can work, it cannot replace the bonding that occurs when we are face to face with our student. Good teachers engage in this eye contact not incidentally, but intentionally. They give their students the attention they deserve and in doing so they are investing in their students. Positive and productive relationships that enhance the school experience, and in turn foster learning, are the returns we get on that investment. It is no accident that most of the missions we construct involve face to face contact with an opportunity for some intentional eye contact that otherwise might not have been part of your week.

4 Habits of Teachers That Have "It" - Part 2 - Smile - Mark Johnson

Intentional use of eye contact can help significantly when building relationships with your students. Just a few seconds of looking into someone's eyes can give them the feeling of comfort and care, and let's them know you are thinking about them and focusing on them. Nothing else matters for that brief moment except them. Teachers who have "it" make this a priority in their lives, because they know that attention is important for their students.

The next "it" factor can be paired along very nicely with eye contact. It is something that, when you give it away, you usually get it in return, almost immediately. It is something that can brighten someone's day and give them a shot of energy, especially when they are feeling sad or tired or alone. It is something that is free and is scientifically proven to give you health benefits and can possibly extend your life. Turn up the corners of your mouth, show your teeth, and you'll see what I mean. Feels good, doesn't it?

I remember when I first got hired as a teacher. I was scared to death. My biggest concern was behavior management. So I did some research and read some articles about the best strategies out there that could help me right off the bat. The one thing I latched on to was this philosophy/mantra: "Don't Smile Until Christmas." For some reason, that made sense to me. If I'm going to set up the rules in the classroom, I'm going to do it right. I'm going to be strict, I'm going to be all business, and the kids are going to know my classroom is a place for work – not fun. My biggest challenge, before reading the behavior management materials, is that I'm a pretty happy guy.

Smiling comes fairly easily for me. In fact, I often run informal experiments out in public and try to smile at as many people as I can, and quietly count how many smiles I get in return. To try and fight against my very nature was harder than I thought it would be, and felt very uncomfortable. But the person who wrote the article was a Doctor of Education, so I figured he knew a lot more than me.

This new plan lasted only two weeks. While writing on the board with my back turned, one of my students responded to a question using a weird voice. While I don't remember what he said, I do remember that I thought it was hilarious, so I started laughing. Instantly I started to panic because I knew this was well before Christmas. I had a long way to go if I was going to make this work. But when I started laughing, the class started laughing, too. I turned around and laughed some more. I saw a classroom full of smiles and laughter. So I gave in to my natural tendencies, and my panic turned to full on laughter, and ended in liberation. The best part is, do you know what I discovered? Mass chaos did not ensue. The students did not revolt. Rules were still followed. Life went on as usual. And everyone was much much happier.

But we're not just talking about smiling when you are happy or in a good mood, because let's be honest – there are things that happen in your day that really make it difficult. And it is okay to be transparent and honest around your students. There are times you will cry with them, or be upset with them, or feel completely exhausted with their behavior. However, as Sam wrote in a previous story, for many of our students school is their "one best place." So while there are times that you may not feel like smiling, remember that some students don't experience much joy when they leave your classroom. For eight hours of their day, we have the power to make it as happy of a place as we possibly can. Even when disciplining a student, we can smile and show them we love them, and will help them learn through the mistakes they may have made.

I mean, think about it? What place do you want to work where there are no smiles? No laughter? I can't think of one. Especially not a school! And this has nothing to do with charisma. You don't have to be particularly charismatic to smile at someone. But a teacher who smiles is a teacher who shows she cares without saying a thing. It is a powerful tool a teacher can use that speaks volumes to a student in a matter of seconds. And those seconds matter more than you know.

4 Habits of Teachers That Have "It" - Part 3 - Physical Contact - Sam Stecher

There is a good chance that I am about to advise no small number of you to go against your instincts. It is also possible that I am going to give some of you permission to engage in behavior you know in your heart to be good but have held back in fear of reproach.

First, let me give you a few reminders of our rationale behind these interventions:

1. We are talking about taking intentional steps to foster positive and productive bonds with our students resulting in greater learning.
2. These interventions are based on ways humans bond.
3. And again, though all parties involved may at some points exhibit behavior that indicates otherwise, both we and our students are human.

With that, take a deep breath and open your mind to the unconventional.

Humans bond through physical contact. It precedes bonding through language by innumerable years. Touch is a fundamental encounter in our human social construction. So, of course, you can foster the bonds we hope to build by intentionally touching your students. Right? Many teachers that have "it" frequently make use of this intervention, effortlessly nurturing their students without even knowing they are doing so. Coaches, some of the best teachers in their own right, seem to be masters at this intervention. I believe it is something that many educators could use intentionally with great results.

Before you completely put on the brakes, let's acknowledge the litigious concerns of advocating physical contact as intentional bonding intervention. I know attorneys. I have heard attorneys utter phrases like, "I advise that you do not engage in any inessential physical contact with students. Furthermore, as you provide training to school communities on classroom climate, I would advise that you do not advocate doing so as an intervention. The only thing worse would be to put it in writing."

You can see how far that advice went with me.

But I think that we have a powerful manner in which we can engage in physical contact with our students while teaching an essential social skill and mitigating litigious inclinations. For the love of Pete, just teach your students how to shake hands and continue to engage in the activity consistently. It is a simple act (like intentional eye contact and smiling) that pays immense dividends for the nominal investment. I can remember when I learned just how important a solid hand shake was in social interactions. When I was a sophomore in high school I had an ankle injury during football season. My father took me to see a trainer at a local university. The trainer I met was from a different generation than mine. He played football in a time when those who elected to participate while wearing a leather helmet were sneered at for being soft. My father introduced me and I extended my hand. Upon grasping my hand the trainer said, "Son, 'for we fix you ankle we need to fix you handshake 'cuz they obviously mo' wrong with you than you father know about. You need to come in, meet at the crease between you thumb and first finger. Take hold all the way 'round the knuckles but don't try and make no dust otta 'em. One or two pumps is enough. It ain't foreplay. We just gettin' to know each other. Clear son?"

Clear indeed. I never forgot that lesson.

I also know that it is a lesson many students never get. That alone is enough reason to engage in the handshake intervention. In doing so you may end up being the person that taught the lesson that allowed a student to find gainful employment. And if this feels right for you, by all means bring in the high fives, the pounds, that pats on the back, etc. If the only thing you do is make sure every one of your students gets one of those every day you will be party to some significant climate interventions.

And now for the disclaimer. Some of you will absolutely not be cool with this. I completely respect that perspective. If this is out of your comfort zone you have my permission to disregard everything I have advocated and rationalized in this article. But with that disregard comes an obligation. You now have an obligation to apply both eye contact and that intentional smile all the more frequently. You can more than make up the missing distance through prodigious use of those two interventions. And fortunately for you, we have one more habit that will assist even further.

4 Habits of Teachers That Have "It" - Part 4 - Time - Mark Johnson

Time. It's one thing we all have in common. Everyone has 24 hours in their day. No more, no less. But when we are speaking of teachers, it feels like they have less time than others. Many of them don't even have time for a bathroom break during the day. They are masters of maximizing every second of their day, making sure even transition times are measured down to the second to protect the learning time they need for their students. If you ask a teacher, they will tell you they don't have any time to spare.

Teachers spend at least 7 hours a day with their students. But this is just an estimate. This doesn't include before school duties or after school activities or coaching or music programs or all of the other things a teacher does for their students. However, teachers who have "it" make sure all this time they spend with their students is an investment towards building and maintaining a positive relationship with them.

One way I tried to spend extra time with my students was during recess. That being said, there are specific ways to monitor a playground. I've even been subjected to training videos on how to use my peripheral vision most effectively when monitoring a large group of students in an open field. How to never converse with a fellow colleague while on the playground. How to walk around the area, always keeping an eye out for anything out of the ordinary, especially horseplay. However, I found the most effective use of my time outside with students was to play with them.

I liked to interact with them on the playground because the way they behaved in the classroom was significantly different than the way they behaved outside. Without the confines of walls and routine, they really opened themselves up. I walked around and joined whatever activity they were doing: jumping rope, playing a game of shoot out, football, swinging, whatever. The kids would get crazy happy when I joined in with them. And monitoring them became that much easier, because most of the time the students would gather around and watch the mayhem or join in. I knew it made a difference with them when parents would tell me the best part of their child's year was when their teacher cut loose and played with them.

Another way for teachers to spend time indirectly with their students is watching them outside of school in extracurricular activities. Have you ever been asked by a student to attend their soccer game, or watch their dance recital, or their speech competition? And when they ask, you immediately start thinking about how busy you are and make excuses about how there is no way you can make it, but you will really try? What I'm suggesting is that you do more than try. All you need to do is make an appearance. Just stand on the sidelines for one quarter of the game. Stand in the back and watch one performance. You don't need to give up your entire night or weekend. Just five minutes will do. The next morning when you tell the student how great you thought they were and say something specific about that event, their eyes will bulge with awe. And even more powerful, if that student catches your eye while you are actually there…that's an investment that might last a lifetime.

In summary: I once heard it said by a speaker at a conference that you have no business complaining about the behavior issues in your classroom if you are not at the door greeting your students every day. That was over ten years ago when I first heard that, and it has stuck with me ever since. It just makes sense. If children arrive to school and see you waiting to welcome them into their classroom, they are much more likely to want to be there, and to start their day off on the right foot.

If you think about it, standing at the door and greeting your students combines all four habits together. Standing at the door and greeting your students means you give them direct **eye contact**, you **smile**, you **touch** them through a handshake, high five or hug, and you spend a moment in **time** with each student individually before the day even begins. If you are a teacher with a classroom, this can happen right outside the door. If you are a principal, it can be by the front doors. If you don't have a classroom, find a high traffic area in the hallway each morning. It doesn't matter where it is. What matters is that you are making a very intentional effort each and every day to make a child's life better, to let them know they matter to you.

You might already feel like you are a teacher who has "it." Why not increase your chances of success with your students by establishing these positive relationship building habits? I know you've heard the old adage: "They don't care about how much you know, until they know how much you care." Whether you agree with it or not, it rings true for many of our students. And that's reason enough for me.

So You Think You Can Teach My Son? - Mark Johnson

My son, Sammy, said he wanted to help me write an article, so he grabbed my computer and typed for a bit. When he handed it back, this is what he had written: "School is very boring. Here, let me prove to you how boring it is –**S**even **C**rap **H**ours **O**f **O**ur Lives."

Now, before you jump to any conclusions or judge my son, let me tell you a little bit about him. First of all, when he wrote this he was a freshman in high school. Secondly, he was a teenager. Thirdly, he thinks he is pretty funny. Last of all, he really does like school, but only on two conditions.

Condition One:
He has to know that the teacher likes him. This has always been the case for him. He will not try in a class if he feels like the teacher does not care about him. He will sit there, fake attention, not contribute, and give the minimal amount of effort required each day. However, on the flip side, if he knows the teacher does like him, he will go out of his way to prove his worth. He will always be to class on time, he will study hard, he will share his thoughts, and he will share funny stories about the class, and about that particular teacher, with me after school.

Condition Two:
He likes to be interested in what he is learning. When he was much younger, he loved football like crazy. He used to collect football cards and read about the players and watch as much football on TV as possible. He could rattle off stats about almost any team and player. He didn't even have to try to remember all of this information. It was just fun for him so it came easy for him. That's exactly the way

it is for him now. The subjects he likes in school, he devours. But if he is bored or doesn't care about what he is learning, it's like pulling teeth to get him to study.

One of these conditions is more important than the other one. If only condition two were in place, Sammy's success would be dependent upon whether or not he liked the subject. Each semester he likes about half of the subjects he is required to take. With those odds, he would only pass half of his classes. But if only condition one were in place, regardless if he liked the subject, he would still work hard because of the relationship he has with his teacher.

I don't think this is exclusively true for my son. I think many students operate under these conditions. And I think most students are craving teachers who like them. Teachers who don't have favorites, but who genuinely care for each and every one of their students. So if you are that kind of a teacher, thank you. Sammy can't wait to get into your class.

The Only Thing a Principal Needs to Know - Mark Johnson

I taught in the classroom for twelve years before I became a principal, which I have been doing for eight years. If you do the math (which isn't that difficult) I have been involved in education as a career for 20 years. I have learned a lot in those years, and I still have plenty left to learn. But there is one thing I know as a principal that has helped me exponentially. It is the one thing that has helped me the most as a leader. It is the only thing I need to know. But I'll get to that in just a bit.

While I was a teacher I had the time of my life. I felt like I was doing exactly what I had been called to do. Everyday I walked into the school and entered my classroom it felt like I was going to my second home. I was so comfortable being around students everyday, and they were comfortable being around me. Many days they didn't want to go out to recess. They would rather stay inside and help me or just talk. Those, of course, were the days when I didn't go out to recess myself and play football or four-square or jump rope with them. I enjoyed every day. Even the challenging ones. I couldn't wait to get to school, and I was sad when the day ended.

Now that I'm a principal I find that I enjoy each day just as much as I did as a teacher. However, my job description has changed considerably. I am now in charge of not only my schedule, but the schedule of each teacher in the building. I have to make budget decisions, implement school-wide discipline, lead meetings, attend meetings, track data, analyze data, conduct walk-throughs, evaluate teachers, and basically know what is happening in and around the building every second of every day. All that being said, I absolutely love what I do.

But too many times, principals begin to separate themselves from the classroom and the life of a teacher as they become bogged down with their own day-to-day responsibilities. They start to make decisions based on the perspective of the office instead of the perspective of the classroom. If you are considering the principalship one day, let me encourage you to jump in and take the plunge. It will be an incredibly rewarding experience. But before you do, let me give you some advice. You will read tons of articles and books and blogs and "The Top 10 Things You Need To Know" about the principalship and being a leader. Most of the things you read will be extremely helpful. But let me tell you right now the only thing a principal needs to know: NEVER, EVER FORGET WHAT IT WAS LIKE TO BE A TEACHER.

That's it. That's all you need to know. Paste it above your door. Write it down on a piece of paper and carry it around. Tattoo it on your arm. Always keep a teacher's perspective, because if you can remember that one simple thing when you need to make decisions that affect teachers and students in your building, you stay on the right path.

#TLAT - Sam Stecher

Let's start this off with an admission of a known character trait and a full disclosure of my hypocrisy. I love the spotlight. The prosecution respectfully submits the following as evidence:

Exhibit A - Sam Stecher has been known to compete in Slam Poetry and perform poems about upper respiratory infections with frequent and explicit references to phlegm.

Exhibit B - Sam Stecher used to be a cage fighter, mostly because to him the saying "two men enter, one man leaves" indicated that everyone would probably be looking at him when all was said and done.

Exhibit C - Have you listened to the Mission Monday podcast? The dude is clearly in love with his own voice.

Guilty. As. Charged.

I'm a showman and a showoff. I love an audience and I love the attention.

Applause?

Yes please.

Laughter?

I am in constant search of a punch line.

Tears?

Oh, are those your heart strings? Did I mention I'm a tug-o-war champion, too? Get ready for some pulling.

So, of course, I became a teacher. Along with the fat contract and wicked good benefits came a captive audience 5 days a week, 6 classes a day, plus the late show when I coached. And I wasn't shy about putting on a show.

"Hello 8th graders. I'm sure you are all here to see me me me."

I had, dare I say, a stage persona.

You know, it worked pretty well some of the time. My personality was suited to this kind of life. And I bet most of my students gleaned some knowledge in between my theatrics. All was well in the "Sam Show."

But then a guy named Dr. Raymond C. Jones ego checked me right into the wall. I was at a workshop he was leading when he smacked me with these words:

"I used to think that teaching was all about entertainment. Then I realized I was competing with Disney and MTV. I don't have the budget or the talent to match them so I will lose the battle for entertainment. But engagement, that's a battle I can win. The difference being, entertainment is all about what I'm doing, and engagement is all about what the student is doing."

Dr. Jones went on to provide a ton of great methods for student engagement that I used for the rest of my teaching career. In fact, I used one again recently with my school board as part of a book study. He's worth a Google search. Go check him out. Beyond the practical application of strategies he provided, that statement above really made me question what I did in the classroom. That questioning led me to some significant realizations. I realized it's not about me. It's about the students. If I came in every day trying to sell myself I would be selling my students short. It's not about what I can show the students about me. It's about what I can get them to see in themselves. I was also selling the profession of teaching short, too. That fat contract didn't say ringmaster or intellectual acrobat or renegade seating chart jockey. It said *teacher*. I didn't need to dress up that title at all. It is one of the most radical, risky, and rewarding careers ever. A teacher is not in the game of mass entertainment. A teacher is in the service of mind expansion. Labeling teaching something it's not is a discredit to what it is.

I know that there are people advocating cultivating the neglected art of "teaching as performance" and I for sure see the value in it. You gotta sell your material a little but the hyperbole is out of hand. Teaching like one's coiffure is en fuego or like you are a posing as a privateer off the coast of Barbados? I question the sustainability. I question the viability of broad application. Most importantly, I question why we would need to sell teaching as something it is not when what it is is so amazing.

As a self confessed but reformed scene stealer in my own classroom, listen to what I say.
Worry less about selling yourself.
Focus on buying into what your students can do.
If you make engaging your students in the learning your priority, do you know what you will be teaching like?
A teacher.

Teach like a teacher.

#TLAT

Competition vs. Cooperation: What is better for our schools? - Mark Johnson

Over one Easter vacation, something happened that I can't get out of my mind. My wife's family conducted the annual egg hunt for all of the children, ranging in ages from seven to seventeen. The plastic eggs were hidden all over the yard, some filled with candy and others filled with various amounts of money. The kids scrambled all over the yard, screaming with delight as their baskets were filling to the brim. When the hunt was over, they all came inside and emptied their eggs onto the floor, looking over the newly found loot.

Grandma had an idea in her head about how this was going to go down. She had a vision of all of the kids emptying their money into one big pile, and in the end, dividing it out equally amongst themselves. It was a good thought, and one that expressed the idea of cooperation. I have to give her credit, because she believes in a world where everyone gets along and we all help each other. Boy, was she ever wrong. When she announced her idea, the looks on the children's faces turned from elation at finding their new treasures, to fear at having to give up what was clearly theirs and theirs alone. In fact, I witnessed one of the younger children pocket some of the money he found, not willing to give up all of his stash. Grandma's vision of cooperation quickly turned to one of competition. They had an inner desire to have more and be better than everyone else around them, so no one agreed to the combining of the money.

This got me thinking about how things run in our education system. It's a system based on competition. We like our schools to be the very best, and with that mindset, unfortunately, comes the need for a rank/order system so we can prove that indeed, some schools are the best. And what about those schools that rank lower on the list? Clearly they aren't doing their jobs. Something must be done about it, and many times what we feel are desperate times should result in desperate measures. There are stories and rumors of school principals being fired, teachers being let go, parents pulling their kids out of one school and placing them in another. But is this really the best way to go?

To be honest, I am a proponent of some levels of competition in education. I actually don't mind that there are charter schools and private schools and public schools. Obviously, someone along the way felt that things in education could be better, so they planned a new way of doing things in schools, and opened up their own school. This idea springboarded into hundreds of schools opening up. This is not a bad thing. Dreaming up better ways to educate our students should be the norm, not the exception.

However, just the very idea of competition implies there is a winner and a loser. This translates to some schools getting to sit at the top of the list, while some are stuck at the bottom. So if a "winning" school wants to keep that distinction, they often feel the need to keep their innovative ideas and teaching strategies to themselves, like the young boy hoarding his money. That's the only way to stay on top. If those schools, or any schools for that matter, share their ideas with others, then what's to become of that? Then all of the schools will sit at the top, and there isn't room at the top for everyone, is there?

But can you imagine if schools not only competed with each other in a healthy way, but also cooperated with each other and pushed each other to get better? In a nutshell, we would all learn more, have more, become greater. And what of the ranking systems? I believe they would become null and void. Is that what we really want? To ALL be great together? To have a nation filled with schools that are all working together for the greater good of students everywhere? I think the way we answer that question defines who we are as an educator. I believe the answer is worth exploring.

Consistent Bed Times and Other Graduation Interventions - Sam Stecher

In 2014 a rather substantial research study received no small amount of press. I say substantial because it surveyed over 10,000 subjects and followed them over the span of 4 years. That scope was one of the elements that made me take notice. The topic of the study was the effect of bedtime on the behavior of children. One of the findings was that children going to bed at 9 at night or later were more likely to have behavior problems. This is unsurprising due to the substantial research available regarding how insufficient sleep impacts children in numerous undesirable ways. What the researchers were surprised by was that an inconsistent bedtime was even more detrimental. Parents and teachers saw more behavioral problems exhibited by children with inconsistent bedtimes than those that were short on sleep.

The research provided no insight into sleep patterns of parents or teachers and the behavior problems they may exhibit, but my anecdotal evidence gathered during parent-teacher conferences leads me to believe that a correlation may exist. Neither of the findings were surprising to me. All of us in education know first hand how problematic both inadequate sleep and inconsistent routine can be for our students. But I think there's more going on here in addition to adequate and consistent sleep as a behavior intervention for children. I think that this is pretty solid evidence that small interventions applied consistently remedy significant concerns. Maybe your child has a habit of earning negative consequences at school. You could try a very stern and impassioned lecture explaining about what is so undesirable about the behavior as well as the duration of imminent grounding if it persists. We all remember just how effective those were in our own upbringing.

Or you could pick one habit, like consistent bedtime, to practice. It should be an attainable habit. It should be nominal but significant. And yes, I know that by definition those two words -nominal but significant- are contradictory. But the small things add up. I believe that too often we make grand and ambitious declarations such as "I am going to lose 30 pounds!" because it is easy to say such things. But we don't focus on the habits that support the goal. What we should be saying is, "I am going to use the stairs at every opportunity." The little things take care of the big things.

Here is a few more declaration don'ts and do's:

Don't say – "I am going to make sure my classroom is the most positive place my students have ever seen every day!"
Do - Greet your students every day at the classroom door.

Don't say - "I will love my job and my coworkers without reservation every day."
Do - Stop in a different fellow teacher's classroom to say "hi" and ask them how they are doing.

One more, because Mark and I prescribe missions about goal setting with some frequency- Don't plan a grand incentive party for a classroom/school goal without validating the daily habits that make the goal attainable. We all need pep talks from time to time. We all need the grand gestures for motivation and to remind us why we do the small things that are important. But pep rallies don't win games. Consistent practice does.

So kids, parents, and teachers - Get to bed on time. It might make all the other small things even easier. And that is when everything falls into place for your goals whether they be for the week, your New Year's resolution, or college admittance.

I Want You To Save A Date - Sam Stecher

At kindergarten graduation, the last chance I had to formally address the parents at the school where I served as principal, this is what I said: "I want you to save a date. It is twelve years from now. I don't know the exact date. But it will be twelve years from now. It's important. Make a note of it. Don't lose sight of it. Keep talking with your children about it. It's important because we are going to do this again. It will be in a different school. Your kids won't be quite as cute as they are today. They will be much taller. And you will be so proud. Twelve years from now let's make sure they have a diploma in their hands."

I didn't have a kindergarten graduation. I met the requirements to be promoted to First Grade but kindergarten graduation was not something we did at Broadview Elementary. It would have been an interesting ceremony to see. If my memory serves me correctly I was in a class of one. I might have had more classmates but it's hard to remember. Broadview was a two-room school house. Students in kindergarten through second grade were housed in one of the rooms so my kindergarten memory can't always sort out who exactly was in kindergarten with me. In addition to the K-2 variables I also had classmates that moved in and out on occasion. I believe that the most peers I ever had in my grade with me during my elementary years was 3 or maybe 4. But I have a pretty distinct memory of showing up the first day of school for kindergarten and being quite the novelty as the entire kindergarten class. Given what would be charitably described as my precocious nature as a child, I ate that attention up. Kindergarten was my jam. And if Broadview Elementary would have seen fit to hold commencement ceremonies for the Kindergarten class of 1979 on the stage in the basement I would have been beaming with delight as the sole honoree. But we didn't. As it turns out I was none the worse for wear.

Both of my parents, Joe and Sally, were high school and college graduates. Both are exceptionally intelligent, hard working, and a bit unconventional. Upon completion of their postsecondary education neither entered the workforce in occupations that were even close to the degrees they had earned. They started a family. They worked the farm where my dad grew up. They worked second and third jobs in kitchens and meat packing plants. My mom eventually worked her way from the kitchen to an administrative position in a nursing home. Under her leadership they set some kind of state record for consecutive perfect scores on state inspections. She also provided a loving environment for a whole lot of people when they needed it most. She also fought through two separate cancer diagnoses successfully. My dad became a lawyer. For three years he ran the family farm while commuting 2 hours a day to attend law school. Eventually served as the U.S. Attorney for Nebraska. I had some good models to follow for success. From Joe and Sally I learned that a job that pays the bills is never beneath you. I learned that getting up early, working hard, and doing more than is expected of you is a pretty powerful combination. I also learned that if you have respectable brain power you owe it to yourself to set goals and put yourself in a position to make use of that gift. Was I set up to graduate high school? You bet. College? No doubt. Was I equipped to handle challenges and failures along the way? They didn't slow Joe and Sally down. They were not going to stop me, either. The absence of a kindergarten graduation ceremony certainly didn't derail me, either.

My experience is not representative of that of the kindergarten students I have served. About all I can count on being the same is that we all started around age 5 or 6. Some have a Joe and Sally. Some have a decidedly different dynamic at home. The obstacles they face and the assets they possess are varied beyond any measure I can perceive or even hope to control. I cannot give each student a Joe and Sally. What I can do is foster a team of teachers that knows every day from kindergarten on is building towards graduation. Every child we serve is a graduate waiting to happen. Every day is progress towards a diploma. Every interaction with a child and with a child's family is a step towards those last few steps across the stage to shake a hand and accept a diploma. We can model and foster the importance, the investment, the work ethic, the value, the grit, and countless other qualities that our students need in our interactions every day.

The kindergarten teachers put up a sign in our gym for the ceremony that read "Graduation Starts With Kindergarten." It surely does.

5 Reasons I Didn't Quit Teaching - Sam Stecher

There is a considerable amount of research out there about why the teachers who don't stick with teaching look for employment in other fields. The reasons revealed are pretty intuitive: low-end compensation, high-end expectations, feelings of isolation, and a myriad of others. Most research of this sort raises some compelling points. And the conclusions drawn are at times valid, and in other instances profoundly flawed. But as I read research of this nature I find my focus drifting from the assertions and presumptions of the articles to my own personal experience. To be more precise I find myself asking why I stayed in the classroom as long as I did.

Just so you know where I am coming from, my classroom teaching experience began in 1997 and lasted until I transitioned into educational administration in 2008. And yes, I am still in education. Though I still hold on to the identity of "teacher" through my role, students and classroom are a bit differently defined. But even with significant overlap of function and motivation between my roles as a teacher and an administrator/consultant, they are decidedly different. Having a school is not having a classroom. A conference ballroom full of teachers in chairs is not a classroom. I left the exclusive privilege of a classroom behind. So for this exercise I am going to focus on what kept me specifically in the classroom for those 11 years. (My transition to administration, aka "The Darkisde," is another topic). With all the easily identifiable reasons, as well as the intangible perceptions that work against longevity in this profession, here is what kept me around:

1)   The part where you actually teach is an absolute blast. Seriously, this part is amazing and we get to engage in it every day. I think sometimes we forget about that part. We get wrapped up in the extra responsibilities, insufficient compensation, social perception, incongruity of accountability in relation to support, and numerous other strikes and we forget that we get to teach, too. Every day we get to be an essential component of that mystical encounter of imparting understanding. I loved that part. If you are even semi-proficient at teaching, most of your students will love learning. Their brains are wired for it. It sounds like a no brainer revelation but teaching was my favorite part of teaching. It is also easy to lose sight of the joy of actual instruction. The opportunity to get to do what I loved most every day amongst the less savory elements of my contractual obligations kept me fulfilled.

2)   I had a hunch I could be pretty good at teaching. I thought I had a knack for this thing. It just felt right. Putting all my classes and field experiences aside I had a gut feeling that a classroom was where I was supposed to be. I believed that if I had the chance to run a class I could be effective. Once I had that chance it was no longer intuition based. The classroom was where I belonged.

3)   I had mentors who told me I was pretty good at teaching. I had several people that validated my hunch. Perhaps the most influential was Ken Mumm. He served as my assistant principal during my first few years as a teacher. Early on he made it very clear that I had what it took to be a good teacher. He also made it very clear I was not at my maximum potential straight out of the gate. He validated what I intuitively knew and where I should be headed. In my last evaluation with him before he retired he

told me, "Sam, you're one hell of a teacher." Something you need to know about Ken - He was one of two people that kept me from quitting my first year of teaching. Such a statement from him, face to face in his office, was a profound validation of what my intuition had told me.

4)   I changed jobs pretty frequently. Though I stayed in the same school system, in fact in the same building, all 11 of those years, I did serve in three separate teaching positions on three distinct middle school teams. Another educator I look up to once said, "It is a fine line between being in groove and in a rut. And after 5 years in the same job it gets more difficult to stay out of the rut." Another one of my mentors also recently told me that he wants to stay in every job for a 3 year term, learn what it has to offer, and move on to the next challenge. I would call it a *rut avoidance career trajectory*. Switching teaching positions was not intentional as a burn out prevention intervention. I just have tendency to seek challenge over comfort. Not everybody is wired that way but in retrospect it has kept me out of the rut.

5)   I loved the content but it didn't define me as a teacher. I loved teaching about the Corps of Discovery. If I could go back in time there is a strong possibility I would join Lewis and Clark on the journey West. That was my favorite topic to teach. But Lewis and Clark do not constitute a school year's worth of instruction. Nor does dividing fractions. Or *Lord of the Flies* for that matter. More than the content I loved the process and the students. Those are the things that brought me to school fired up about my service. I was a teacher first. It just so happened that I was a history teacher. I think if your primary passion is the content as opposed to who you serve and the

process of teaching, you are setting yourself up for burnout.

We have a tendency in our profession to focus on what is not worth it. I don't mean to disregard our challenges. I believe we have fundamental components of our educational system that need immediate attention and an informed remedy. However, don't forget why you personally stay in the classroom and in education. In fact make your own list. Share this and your reasons with your peers as well.

So You Want To Be A Teacher? - Mark Johnson

Teaching is the most important profession in the world. I may be biased in my opinion, but I'm also right. There is no other profession that touches more lives than teaching. The difference a teacher can make can span across generations. Others have careers and have pursued their dreams because of the education they received, and that education they received was most likely the result of a teacher. Even the Bible has some words about the teaching profession: "Not many of you should become teachers, my brothers, for you know that we who teach will be judged with greater strictness." (James 3:1)

One of my favorite poems is titled "so you want to be a writer" by Charles Bukowski. If you have not read it, you can find it pretty easily with a web search. It is a wonderful challenge to those who want to pursue writing as a career. I have used the idea behind that poem to write my own simple challenge to those that think they want to enter the teaching profession. I hope you enjoy it.

So You Want To Be A Teacher?

If you want a job where you work 8:00 – 5:00,
then don't do it.
There are plenty of other opportunities
out there where you can keep your work day
nice and tidy.

If you are becoming a teacher because you
like the content you will be teaching
you get excited about hearing the sound of your own voice
sharing your knowledge with the masses,

then don't do it.
There are other places you can go and talk about
things you know,
and plenty of other people who might want to hear it.
But a classroom of students year after year
will not be one of those places.

If you are becoming a teacher because you
don't know what else to do,
don't do it.
The future of our children can't afford the time
it might take you to figure out what to do
with your own life.

If you are getting into teaching because you
"just love kids,"
then that's a good beginning.
If you like your students
you are well on your way to
building positive relationships.
And it might buy you a few years,
but that alone is not going to carry you through
an entire career.

If you were inspired by a teacher
when you were younger,
a teacher that made you question the world,
made you think,
made you laugh,
made you cry,
made you want to become a better version of
yourself,
then hold onto that.
Inspiration is a great way to start any adventure.

You will know you
really want to be a teacher
because you will feel a passion
burning inside of you that you have never felt before.
When every decision you make is
filtered through the question -
Is this the best thing for my students?
When you can't imagine yourself doing
anything else
in the whole word.
You will know when you can't wait to
wake up in the morning,
when you can't sleep at night,
when your every minute is consumed
by how you can help your students
learn more,
be more,
achieve more.
That's when you will know.
And when you know,
don't ever stop
knowing.

Made in the USA
Las Vegas, NV
09 September 2022

55005205R00049